A Schizophrenic Is Never Lonely Poems

Steve Baba

Crimson Milk Press
San Francisco

Copyright © 2015 Steve Baba

Cover design by Steve Baba

Ways to contact the author:
www.stevebaba.com
facebook.com/stevebaba
twitter.com/stevenhbaba

First printing, April 2015
Printed in the USA

ISBN: 0692422072
ISBN-13: 978-0692422076

Table Of Contents

I.

II.

III.

For Grandma and Grandpa Suzui. How I miss you so.

I.

Motorcycle Crash

please let me know
as soon as you know
thank you

the white tiles squeaked
under your sneakers

the wafting cigarette smoke
littering the no smoking zone

haven't shaved in 6 days
looks like hell
only coffee can keep him sane

nobody dared talk about the accident
he ran into a tree
one of his ribs punctured his heart

surgery
too long
about 8 hours

there was no indication from the
white coats whether he would
live or die

poor kristina
they just got married
and she found out she was
pregnant

nobody knows
nobody knows

there will be scars
seen and unseen

Daunting Circumstances

congealing corporation
situation nil

bought bought
the cd today
dee bee dee bee day

water seven
desert five
death valley -226

count the sheep
listen to the wing
dawdling in pig's blood

how many sheep?
499
too many too many

beating
hovering on the wind
feathers brown and grey

bathe in it
drink it
wash your mouth in it

salacious as it might be
have sex with your best friend
i'm sure she won't mind

Is This Racism?

check your coat
at the door

frogs will jump
out of the pockets

the daily news
yellow journalism
who reads this stuff anyways?

a crash course
in boiling the eggs

a draft of a novel
bitten by writer's block

don't bite your nails
you'll chip your teeth
that's how old you are

preen your afro
it looks like cotton candy
but smells like kiwi

empty your purse
don't let the lady finger tampon
click onto the floor

beat the sleep
cut the vein
wallow in gravy

Embarrassed

the phases of blue
distort under the bridge
and over the bridge

how i love those smooth
bare legs
so sexy!

when i grow up i want grow into
a 320 pound offensive lineman

the only offensive thing about me
is my bad breath

go ahead and snore
the bar is open at 6 am

please please
let the deaf girl like me

i feel sorry for those in need
goodbye cigarettes

wake the mind with caffeine
make it go to sleep with tryptophan

can you say blushing?
animals rarely if ever
get embarrassed

climb the totem pole
and wreck the top idol

Staring Deep

i hate how my face
tells the truth
when i look in the mirror

those black eyes
like volcanic ash
no shining

that overdrawn nose
it spites
it mocks tomatoes

and those thick pale lips
not for kissing
not for speaking

my sadness comes from
deep within
lungs tired from smoking too much

need a shave
need new eyebrows
that doesn't impress me much

wait
i just saw a glimmer
was that just the light?
was that the fly that landed
on my shoulder?

i forgot that i needed
a hug from my shadow

i forgot that i needed
to hide the bags
from the nightmares

Broken Strings

fish in the engine
ice in the vents

a paper shredder
turns on and off
where are the extension cords?

the car is stalled
it won't work because
the hot water
won't keep it going anymore

lollipops on the windowsill
butterflies dead in a corner

she wanted to hit something
what she didn't know is she already did

with a black eye
he sat down on the broken springs
and wiped a droplet of sweat
that was threatening to go into his pupil
people would think he was crying

one day
two nights
three weeks
four months
five years

have things changed?
or have they stayed the same?

San Francisco Daze

calm calm calm

the lake beckons for noise
any kind of noise

someone blows
their nose into a tissue
then throws it to the curb

coins jingle
enough for the bus
all the way to embarcadero

wah wah
i want my way

wah wah
i want my way

ups has stopped delivering
what stopped saturn from
shedding its rings?

a baseball bat
turns into a weapon

a baseball
turns into a projectile

Do You Dare?

this coffee is tasteless
did you dip it in vegetable oil?

a novel half open
page 156
the main character
sweating to find his
lost bank account number

this biscuit is wet
did you spill rose water on it?

dark room
darker face
the black is still coming
is still coming

wait for it
here it is
the forsaken man

who brought sadness
to my heart
he had the secret well
scripted in his journal

i don't know
whether the grass
is green or yellow

it still needs care
or the dogs will dig holes in it
from morning to night

Dank, Dark, Dastardly

she was like a penny
without the shine

he was a glass of cold
grapefruit juice

she was a mirror
that was cracked in the middle

he was the dim light
in the dirty bathroom

she was a cloud that seemed
dizzy in the pale sunshine

he was melancholia
waiting for the right time

to collide
and end it all

she was a piece of a necklace
that broke when he yanked it off her neck

he was a scratched disc
but the movie still played

she left the keys on the table
you open the door

she caught a cold in the dark
he jumped on the bed

with sugar
eating his brain

Public Transportation

the 14
goes all the way to
embarcadero

i get on and smell
urine and croissants

there is a small nuclear family
in the front
they are speaking spanish

then we start
slowly at first but then
a little faster

on off
on off
the people change

i see blurs of bodies
and the constant beep
of the
stop requested sign

24th and mission
there are plenty of shadows here
even in the blight of the sun

Reach Far And Wide

nose itches
eyes twitch

a mermaid sings
she wears a golden ring

dogs chase the convict
and then he lit a cigarette

she read a magazine
with lots of women in it
ought to stop and think about
the wind that is coming through the
screen door

mock me mock me
i don't care if you are blind
i am glad you can't see

the hay goes unstacked
the latte is still warm

dry tongue
there is no love
neither here
nor there

He, Who Thought He Was God

the smirk on his face
betrayed 6,000,000 people
in europe

his mustache twitched
when he heard wagner

the eagle flew above him
it was a sign
blue and blonde the captive colors
the only colors

pink
a limp
a low i.q.
and you were sent to
the places where nobody
would want to go
even me or you

black stripes
white stripes
the mud clung to their soles
the sadness clung to their souls

enter the chamber
water or gas?
you didn't know until it
was too late

they dried out in the winter sun
then put into those human ovens
ashes over the city
ashes over the city

We Are Protestant, We Are Catholic

the bombs went off
in the middle of downtown
37 dead
120 wounded

when they held the funerals
the flag draped over their coffins
even the man with a gun
held it tight against his chest

the dirt turned blue
from the shoe polish

another man
got his throat cut
when someone with a mask
broke into his house

he was listening to mozart
and drinking tea
after a long day driving
his taxi

those poor children
seeing it all
as the fire in the fireplace crackled

it never went away
even after the treaty
violence still in their hearts

Death In Rwanda

bodies float down the river
it has been a long time since it
hasn't smelled of death

missing arms
missing legs
missing ears

the terror on their faces
still frozen

that church
where they all died
he said it would be alright
but he lied

stains of blood
on the streets
on the concrete
on the just grown grass

that plane went down
i don't know if it was sunny
or rainy

but it crashed to the ground
without a scream
without a yell

Aren't We All?

yellow bastards
black bastards

his first word
when he was born
was

nigger

the second word was

jap

and the third was

chink

when he ordered asian food
he would desperately
roll his tongue when the letter
l was spoken

he threw those black bastards
into bogs

he hanged them on gnarled old
oak trees

kicked at those yellow bastards
good for nothings
he would think to himself

i would drown them all
i would curse them all

they don't belong here
they don't deserve to have
our privileges

He Made The Right Choice, They Didn't

bloody face
broken nose
broken ribs

they had no mercy
in their bones
just because he loved men

men in pantyhose
men in dresses
men with too much makeup

he slept with them all
lucky not to have gotten
the killer virus

he couldn't speak
after he healed

scared at his shadow
scared at the shaved heads

even at the rec center
he couldn't see straight

the mop
sloshing in the bucket
no dirt could be
cleaned up off the floor

but he continued
to love men

some with thin arms
some with thin waists

his heart never betrayed him
that he was born this way
born this way

he never hung out at that
bar again

the alley was too dark
the blaze of hate still
burning in their minds

The Jewish Purge

kristallnacht
oh why did it happen?

the date is 9 november
at 12:32 am

the glass flies
the doors broken down
the shots fired out

in the distance
mozart is playing
on the piano

shouts in german
the faces go flush
diamonds in bread
devoured before the
lights go out

dirty
bastard
dirty bastards
they yell

the girl in the red
dress runs down the street
crunch crunch

this is just the start
until 10 november

and many will die
many will suffer
many will be dispossessed

America In Action

she spread her legs
as the flies lingered

a vase full of daisies
a dead rat in the soda can

itchy eye
red eye
darts fly out

a knife rests on the counter
it has tasted many things
the last thing an onion

what is wrong with arizona?
first not allowing the holiday of a hero
the next putting flashlights into
the eyes of the undocumented

thank you washington
thank you colorado

even though both are far away
from each other

it's okay to heal yourself
with green bud

En Route To Australia

the refugees
refused to turn back
even though most were seasick

urine flowed freely on the deck
scraps of banana peels scattered

the babies
those cries of anguish
but to a better place

when the fishing boat came
they were relieved
saved at last

arms and legs
tangled in the nets

sore muscles
dry skin

even the sea was sick of them
they should be on land
not water

a warm blanket
some chilled water

the fish didn't envy them
that day

War Is Hell

he was in the army
sergeant major
he led his men

when they died
it was like lighting
a match

they held their violence
they carried their survival

when the parachutes came down
some broke their necks

mud and darkness
mud and dawn
mud and twilight

they the ones who
slew jews

they the ones who
created this maelstrom

and we the stars
in a play we didn't want to
be in

but we had to anyway
lead on
lead on

and let us let go of death
and let us let go of oppression

Long Live The South!

he hanged from the tree
the one that had served those
white folks some sort of control

flies buzzed around his open eyes
a bird pecked at his cheek

he was only 16 years old
and he was caught kissing a
white girl on the way home from school

her mom caught them in the act
her husband the grand wizard

the poor boy tried to run away
but the police knew where he lived

they threw him through the
screen door of his home
as his mom gripped a handkerchief sobbing

that word
the one i won't utter here
you know the one

they called him a dirty
they called him a crazy

The Slaves Are Heroes

they toiled in the heat
of the day with no breaks

blisters on their fingers
sweat dripping and dripping

to pass away the torture
they sang songs
mostly to god

they couldn't read or write
the only implement they knew
was the whip

she was 10 years old
and she wanted a different life

she heard of that special railroad
that would take people up north

so she stole a little money
from her dad

she made a coat from
burlap bags and straw

two weeks and she would be gone
gone from the torment
and that awful heat

her voice got stronger
the more she sang

her back straighter
after the long work

I'm Sorry That The World Is This Way

he falls into the dumpster
and scrapes his elbow
but he finds some old
pieces of chicken

well worth the pain

he digs and sees something shiny
a nickel perhaps
he pockets it without a thought

a dirty brown sweater
with holes under the arms

this he could use
especially since
the nights were getting colder

then a bang
and another

a baton tells him to
get out
get out now

he slowly gets out
and looks at the ground

the officer smirks
and tells him to move along

he shuffles away
and wonders if his face has grease on it

lights a smoke
his next to last one
has to make it last

A Veteran Gone Crazy

i'm a gonna be a nutjob
and bathe in urine

i'm a gonna eat roses
and hope my heart caresses
the petals

i'm a gonna walk barefoot
on the seething asphalt

she told me never
to defy her

i did and she
burned my tongue

so much for calling her a bitch
so i flipped her off instead

she took a knife and cut
that sucker right off

guess i should be lucky
that she didn't cut off
something more important

i'm a gonna
slide down the sidewalk
and eat squished snails

i'm a gonna soil my pants
and let a gerbil go inside

i'm a gonna share my
shining crazy shopping cart
with you

Trying to Live With Dignity

he puts his ear to the brown
paper bag and listens to nothing

the symphony has stopped
the wind has died down

he kicks that bag down the street
and whistles that familiar tune
the one he used to hear on the radio
back in 1986

his shirt dirty and smelly
his jeans torn
his shoes scuffed and tattered

why does he have to eat
out of a dumpster?

why does he wander the streets
as if he were in his living room?

he has no home
it was burned down long ago
but still he goes on

which way is the light?
up above or down below?

his stomach grumbles
it is time to check the trash again

where are the keys
to unlock the front door?

there is no front door
i am sorry to say

Another Victim

he contracted aids
on his 34th birthday

it was 1984
and he had just finished reading
orwell

his phone rang
it was his best friend's brother
want to come and join us
for dinner? he asked

he said yes
and put the receiver down

changed into some fresh clothes
and he even drove himself there

there was bobby and louis
joe and doug

they had dinner at a nice if cheap
restaurant and had a lot of red wine

everyone went home except for doug
doug took him home and took off his clothes

Gorky Park

shake the tree
and make the sorrow
come out in bunches

drag the body
and take the wallet
and keys

he was not alive
when they finally found him
his body with tears and rips
of flesh all over

no identification
no face (it was sliced off)
no fingertips (these were cut off)

the garden that they found
him in was so tranquil
how could anyone be so brutal?

in russia it was usually very cold
but today it was 18 C
and that was an anomaly
especially since it was
the middle of winter

so this mystery
of this man
or was it a mystery?

they didn't know
what to do
except bring in her

she could feel things
she read things in the air

A Rocky Affair

i don't know
whether to say hello
or goodbye

you told me something
was growing
wait until the 9th month

just like beethoven's 9th
it would come out with applause

i don't remember what night
we finally connected the dots
but it was probably early this year

ding dong
i'd better answer that
or will it be your husband?

the dogs snarled at the door
nope
just the mailman with a
certified letter

i can wipe the sweat from
my upper lip now

boy do i need a drink
and i'm not talking about
water or juice

A Fatal Pool Incident

he wouldn't have died if
only you watched him from the back porch

his lungs full of goldfish
the stingray laughed

when dad came home
and found out
he was pissed and then sad

why? why?
there is no why
only what happened

the screen door stayed locked
from now on
my sister and me
staring out towards the cement

we folded his clothes
we put his toys away
mom made his bed

it stayed that way for
a couple months
then mom got tired
and put some pills in her mouth

The Damn Thing Is Stuck To Us

we will miss the children
when the drought ends

we waste half of our food
into the garbage can

the sun also rises
the moon so envious she
shows us her pockmarked face

we will never end violence
against women
but we must try

we must try

we are against any kind of war
no more bullets
no more bombs

not recycling is like
the grinch on christmas eve

global warming
has caused the world
to melt and melt

goodbye yellow brick road
and don't forget the lollipops

II.

Irrational Violence

irrational
a word that they used
so often
that the seattle rain
liked it

a computer blinking words
a baby sucking on a bottle
a jacket that was left unclaimed on
the wooden chair

they would take bats
and beat the homeless

they would spit and yell
the curses stronger and stronger
with every new victim

hell was here
not below

and they brought the heat
they brought the hate
and satan was happy again

he would have some new disciples
in 20 year's time
god wouldn't let them live that long

Tragedy On The River

catastrophe on the river
a young boy drowned

he was watching the
steamboats going up
and down

the water was murky brown
the cattails reaching
for the shore

it was midday
and his mother was
at work

she was a waitress
getting paid little
except for on the side

he drank milk
and had some toast
before he went to the water

so he died with
a full stomach

when his body was found
it was blue and bloated

a fisherman found the body
he caught him on the line

Tourism For Junkies

false god
happy god

what they don't know will
happen to themselves

when the machines
turn off
they will be absent

or deep beneath the ground
with the mercury

said something
but could not hear
tired are their chests

vibrating hand
a stray lazy green eye
the strike of the century

walgreens is open 24 hours
the banks are open on saturday
remember when the city
center shut down after dark?

candles and letters
but no legacy
too bad too bad

Changes In The Air

the earth screeches
diamonds fall like rain
into the ground

a green sun
still warms
but will soon be gone

eyes hide
like a solar eclipse

where the men
go nobody knows

maybe to the bars
maybe under some shade
maybe to their whores

a broken piece of wood
lies on the river
drifting away
drifting away

when fall comes
they will all be ears

listening to the last of
the crows

listening to the coo
of the lonely dove

Honking Horns

sweet tooth
the coming tidal waves
will cover the warmth
that barely touches my chest

i hear a cough
i hear a sigh

running shoes
a dripping nose
washington won the war

no place that far
except for the cold whiskey
in ice

she sits across the way
reading a book
shooting glances my way

beep beep
the alarm goes off
time to wake up to
the sounds of honking horns
don't they have something
better to do with their lives?

i know what just kidding means
but i don't follow it because
i want to believe in magic

wanted to talk to you this morning
wanted to offer you this peace pipe
wanted to give you a newspaper
where my obituary was in it

Dark Deeds

everything is blurry
as if you were looking into
the flames of a fire

can't discern
can't discern

the smoke rises
like the bile in your throat

hangnail
throbbing pain
the pain is too much

white hair
like limp noodles
nobody wants to touch them

ears plugged
the sad face turns into
a mean face

try to grab the blackness of
the evil tones of ac/dc
did they really worship the devil?

chemical spill
milk spills
the sleet is heavy

broken branches
broken arm
casual smile   .

he will forget everything
except his brother
who fought all his wars for him

Awash In Detritus

a single grain of salt
on your upper lip

you better lick it off
or the record will skip

the pimple on your
left cheek
is still angry

don't squeeze it
or the picture will fade

the car is rusting
let it rust
it's already dead anyways

there is a stain on your dress
no you didn't
no you didn't

pick up the box of tissues
you will need them soon
eating habaneros

twitch twitch
just relax
and have a cup of wine

don't tell me what to do
i am my own cricket
i can make noise if i want to

The Letter

he limped down the hallway
ba dum click
ba dum click

he walked in darkness
never liked the light anyways

opened the door and sat down
the letter still unopened

she rolled over and asked
him if he was okay

he grunted
no need for words at this hour

she rolled back
and snored peacefully

the address on the envelope
was from the philippines
mailed on the 29th of february

that was their anniversary
and they did it as a kind of joke

he took a tissue and wiped his nose
the cough had gone away for a while
but it would be back

For William Stafford

mr. stafford
i understand you now

stand with the oppressed
but don't raise a finger

keep your hands unclenched
keep your eyes clear

but watch out behind you
they'll try there first

digging ditches
and making trails

you listened to the wind
and remembered how free you were
before the war

mr. stafford
thank you very much

you have taught me well
the gun butt may hit me in the
back of the head

the thousands of feet may
kick me in the stomach

but i won't let the blood
make me regret about violence

Insults

tongue too sore
from eating too many
sunflower seeds

cheeks raw with salt

the dreams have come
back again

she with the smirk
and angry green eyes

telling me she is better
than me

to do my work
and shut up

then the dark spot on the
floor
it starts creeping towards me

i think it's a cloak
with a monster's mentality

and i suddenly feel a pop
in my heart

i have let her go
one too many times

the cheese is moldy
the milk sour

then smiles
without sarcasm

without bitterness
without guilt

her skin turns into snakes
her arms octopus tentacles

this is the dream of the twilight
as the ativan works
in my blood
in my head

What Violence Is

the inferior
catches up with the superior

a policeman
waves through
traffic in the busy intersection

they come out from
their hidden spaces

cockroaches and rats
their pets
their companions

they look up at the high rises
and do not wish to be in them

a man stands on a soapbox
and sings an aria
his clothes dirty and made
of holes

briefcases and suits
they will all become dirty too
when the sun disappears

extra napkins
spilt milk
a child figures out
what violence is

Her Bad Habit

she flitted from man to man
never satisfied
always hungry

booze
cigarettes
cocaine
madness

not necessarily in that order

she knew the streets well
poor tom without a home in
alley #1

daisy the well endowed hooker
whose face was coming off
too much makeup

her feet always hurt
when she walked across town
to see manny

he the sugardaddy
with gallons of whiskey
and a loveable parrot
named salty

she had a run in her stocking that morning
when they found tom in the garbage can
lifeless
without hope

he had suffered a heart attack
somewhere around 3 am
looking for last night's dinner

the streets are sad
the people insensitive
and she goes on
with a feather in her cap

A Skyscraper

the buildings are like
weeds
still tall
still growing

the window washers
apply cream cheese to the
chocolate covered windows

wipe wipe
they lick the squeegees
and fart loudly over the
countless men and women
that walk below them

she looks out
and can finally see the
rapist walking on the street
he doesn't know that soon
his head will explode

the catastrophic exam
was easy to her
but the others

they cried
they cried

and all the pens and pencils
turned into dust
turned into ash

Digging Deep

he pulled at his beard
taking out the dirt and coffee grounds

then he opened his mouth
and put a stone on his tongue

he walked on stilts
and tripped on an old dirty doll

then he tried to fix
his bloody broken nose

it was a mistake
that the sun decided to climb
into the sky today

bitter orange peel
slippery banana peel
fallow screams of a little child

spit out the seeds
savor the sweet of the grass
reject the love note on the wall

he went into the house
trying to avoid the heat
of midday

the newspaper was still on the driveway
rubber band gooey
the ink starting to run

Broken Sleep

so the sleep doesn't
come except for hallucinating
dreams with sweat and
rapid heartbeat

he offers you a cigarette
you agree
you take a few puffs
and then you are done

she puts toast on the plate
and butters it
you eat it
you are satisfied

you still have broken dreams
when it is 4:30 am
you see frogs rain
down on the ground

orange juice
bleeds through your cut wrists
your beard is scraggly and dirty
hunger is the last thing to think about

red dot
steeping black tea
the ocean wanders
she still holds the key to the mystery

if you wake up you will feel groggy
you will feel drunk
was all that wine worth it?

Payment

the side of the head
feels dashes and asterisks

smoking menthol
smooth out the lumps

a cell phone rings 3 times
he answers it
no one on the other line

was it always strawberries
and cream?

more like asphalt and mud
a yellow line dividing
their love

pay for the tune up
pay with teeth and fingernails

when the lady with the
leather miniskirt walks by
heads turn

dawn
the overcast skies
hide the light

i can't see her clearly
she looks like an angel
she looks like a demon

There You Go

he says to
throw me a bone
i say i don't have one
to throw

the coins jingle in
his pocket
only for coffee
only for coffee

a glass of orange juice
sits on the bare counter
i smell cigarettes
i smell dissent

he squeaks as he walks
across the tiled floor
bought some vodka
for the ensuing madness

why is it that everyone
seems to stare at me when
i flush at the sound of laughter?
someone is mocking me
someone is mocking me

how are you?
i'm doing well
but until tomorrow
then i'll be sober

crush the ants
lift the glasses up
until they say it's ok
then fall down in a heap

saying
it's not good
it's not bad

Unbelievable Vision

anxious about something
anxious about nothing

the coffee tingles
the nicotine awakens

a beautiful nightmare
scars on the cheeks
purple faces
dripping faces
daggers for teeth

the bacon fries
the eggs boil
the potatoes bake

but even after breakfast
you still have chills

paprika
sneezing a few times
trying to clear the head

a memory of that
dark cave
the one you didn't want to
go into

so scared
so scared

and that stench
a mix of shit
and dead bodies

Taqueria

burrito with
cheese
beans
rice and
carne asada

a pacifico
to wash it down your
unfit throat

what are you doing today?
i don't know
pero me gusta ir
al biblioteca
para pedir prestado libros

the mexican waitress
has a plastic face
beautiful but plastic

she has dd breasts
and shiny legs

i slip my number with
the bill
i hope she calls me

how are you?
mucho mejor que ayer

i will bring you a cupcake
it is your birthday
you are 33 today

Aftertaste Of Garlic

he punches his fists
into the sky

a sky that looked like
the painting
the sower

green moon
bring me luck
bring me a relationship

the hot cocoa
is still hot
but not as hot
as a minute ago

aftertaste of garlic
on the tongue

i shouldn't have had that
in my spaghetti
now i'll get heartburn

i can't be at two places
at once
so i'll be here amongst the tigers

they are not hungry
thank goodness for that
they act like a cat
times 1,000

Night Life

the creaking upstairs is
getting worse

i'm going to complain
about the mice that live
above me

poor baby
crying all night long
she is as hot as a piece
of burning coal

she is still angry at her gums
ice cubes ice cubes
the lit cigarette a detriment

so many soiled diapers
all that formula
making it easy for her to defecate

mom and dad
are worried
why the screaming
at 3:22 am?

mary ann
you know your name now
you turn your head to me
when i say your name

Baby Daniel

what a mess
the diapers pile up
as the flies multiply

milk stains on the shirt
her nipples are showing
baby cries because it is hungry

da-da
ma-ma

the dinosaurs keep him
company when the lights go out

the stroller is cold now
he was in it just 10 minutes ago
but the sweat has dried

she drinks some coffee
because he will wake up soon
and it is the bad breaking dawn

music
the kind they play on the
classical radio station
mellow yet dramatic

she sighs
and wonders if she
wasn't a mother anymore

but he was that last bit of sunshine
right before a downpour
she would be lost without him

Temptation

he blows through
his lips
like air leaking out of a tire

the devil asks
if he wants to live
to a hundred and fifty

or if he wants
as much money
as bill gates

he rubs his face
with calloused hands

wasn't he tempted
once before?

he touches
his tie

the half eaten apple
on the ground next
to the hoof

the devil smirks
and already knows the answer

the same answer
since two thousand
years ago

Inner Fear, Outer Fear

fear comes at
the most uncommon times

reading a book
about a murderer

seeing that earthquake
again and again

you know the one
that happened in '89

when dolly was born
who would have thought?

an icepick in the hands
of an amateur

stop the train
fill the bathtub

the little people are here
to cause much trouble

jerk jerk
the circle jerk

urine didn't taste as good
as the leftovers from yesterday

A Lonely Death

i am sorry to say he didn't make it
the stress was too much

someone peeled off his coat
and took many bites out of him

already bruised
now swimming in blood
nobody feels sorry for him

he had no friends
even though he lived
with a bunch of people

he had many cousins
even had some brothers
and sisters

but they didn't care
because the same thing
would happen to them

one time his sister got cut up
by knives

a brother turned black
and rotted away

the was no escape
they were grown up to be consumed
or left to die

their shelf life was brief
and painful

The Insane Inhabit The Earth

she sits by herself
and mumbles in
the paper bag carrying her thoughts

walking with a limp
varicose anger
throbs and throbs

people turn up their noses
she doesn't mean anything
she is just a dirty animal

a little girl
with happy blonde curls
gives her a dollar

but money is just a
piece of paper
just as green as her insanity

her hair like a shag carpet
her face like a torn map
her feet like a couple of clubs

so sorry she whispers
god hasn't answered her prayers
in 20 years

Domestic Happenings

look at him in the eye
like when you were a baby

even then you
gazed at him like
a hawk and its prey

no more fists
no more insults

the kitchen floor
is cold under your bare feet

the lines in his
forehead deepen

will you stand up
for yourself
this time?

when you had bruises
on your arm
nobody told

when you had a black eye
nobody told

he shunned broken bones
but he made your nose swell

III.

Scoff

what was it?
a fish on a hook?
a rat poisoned?

the weeds are as high
as my nephew
he's 3 feet tall

when the toast is done
my sister adds butter
and cinnamon

unshaven
unshowered
always bursting

he rubs his eyes
they are sore from
reading the too hard book

no more getting high
no more sleeping in
no more hiding food

he mops the floor
with bleach
the tiles shine in the light

i don't understand
the smoke is too enticing
i have to quit or else

Indentured Servant

insert funny word here

laugh

insert angry word here

red

insert sad word here

despair

insert happy word here

elation

i walked the world without
any money
without any love close to
my heart

she was but a dream
a dream that i had every night
the answers are with her

tears

a good or bad thing?

doom

definitely an omen

the road was long and windy
sometimes the wind blew
so fiercely

that i had to sleep with my eyes
half closed

Guilty Or Not Guilty?

i don't make it easy
you have to watch me when
i undress

the stillness in the air
makes you feel full of regret

why?
did you do something wrong?

you went out that night
without me

did you kiss someone?
another man?

no you say
another girl

she was so soft
no whiskers
no rough skin

i think i'll be with her
you say

i shrug my bare shoulders
and take a towel out of the closet

Zenith

when the skies turn blue and black
where will you be?

the light of the rose is still
alive with happiness

goodbye bitterness
goodbye heartache

i will be there for the duration
i will be there for the little daisy
that is perched in your hair

this is the time
when i should not be this happy
but i am
but i am

my face sits in a tree
watching for you to pass
and bring the goodness
of humanity to me

the worry lines fade
the stomach feels full
the daunting task of saying
those three little words
a lot easier for my tongue

don't talk ill of the bad things
do talk good of the good things

when my feelings reach the zenith
i will make sure
that i catch the wind
and spell love on the small
gold leaves

Chopsticks Behind His Ears

chinatown 1983
i saw the dragons
i ate the fortune cookies

but i threw away the fortune
how would it know
what would happen in my life?

a single mom
holding one cherub in one arm
carrying a purse in the other

she slipped on some
chow fun
and broke her ankle

crackle crackle
the fireworks scared
the ghosts from
their hiding places

a man with a stain on
his groin
chopsticks behind his ears

the jade statue stared
at those gweilo
they couldn't figure out
how much it cost

bruce lee was my hero
he with the body of a string bean
he with the coals for eyes

Frida And Diego

bend the bars
bend your will

the newspaper has
your face on the front page

what do you think will
happen when the
monsters come out from
behind the lengthy shadows?

a glass of milk cold
a mug of hot chocolate
a cup of black coffee hot

when the wind blows
there is only the rustle of
the tree branches

no voices
no creaking
no sabotage

a picture of diego rivera
is on the pink plastered wall
why did he cheat on his women?
he wasn't that good looking

the ear is severed
and put into the envelope
destination rachel

she always loved him
all 300 pounds of him
to the end

Irritated

i ate already!
thank you

the smoke leaves my ears
and drifts into my eyes

the mug is hot
dark and cloudy
with tea and cream

i am not that hot new chick
i am the old crone with
breasts hanging down to my waist

hello
she says as she
gets up from the table

the baby cries
the baby cries

trying to hide the wrinkles
trying to hide the limp in her step

click click
the door unlocks

three scoops of sugar
a dash of cinnamon

Clogged

ears clogged
chest clogged
nose clogged

the leopard sheds its spots
as if it were a snake shedding
its skin

wave goodbye to the people
they'll never see you again
sunk at sea

why does the ghost give
you chills at night?
a thousand nail points to the temple

i am an open book
read the passage where i get killed
or when the sun explodes

drums beat
heart beats
knocking on the front door

that old man
sipping his lemonade
his wife died two years ago

Thief And Scoundrel

he stole
he cajoled
he bartered

the first words
out of his mouth were

do you have a cigarette?

the smell of farts everywhere
the iron skillet fried his
long black hair

why green?
why tanned?

the hummingbird necklace
was lost forever

fat woman
skinny woman
ugly woman
old woman

he drove all the time
he always bought pot from
the same dealer

and when he missed
a step on the stairs
he felt fear for the first time

Bloom

the stars are staring at the ground
they want to see the seeds grow into
the trees and flowers

they never see them because they
only come out at night

like a boy growing into a man
the oak tree is going to be big

the daisies will smile
the daffodils will behold the sun

i must be cautious
or something unwise will
happen to me

as the limes on the branches
weigh down

as the roses make the air
smell fragrant

the moments i have now
are going to leave as soon
as they have arrived

the stars are listening to the cicadas
blink and weave

To Understand

don't lose it
not now not ever

she gave you this brass key
she said it would open anything

but you could only use it three times

the first was on your mind
you couldn't understand why you
felt this way

people calling you gay
calling you fag
calling you homo

you never found out
but you got to see something beautiful
a pair of white butterflies
escaped through the entrance

the second was the water
beneath your feet

where was the dirt?
you never saw any
not in your lifetime at least

in front of your eyes you
saw these pieces of ice melting
the water rose

and the land disappeared

you don't know why it happened
but another beautiful thing occurred
a pod of blue whales glided by

and the third and final lock
was a book you were reading and
finished recently

why did the madman get away
with all that evil?
this story was never told to children

you saw a mustache
a black one
hang in the air

and then some horns
black too

finally a forked tail
this was red by the way
and so he was revealed
to the earth

Sticky

suddenly the eggs were vulnerable
weasels possums raccoons
where the cold air was

they pecked at the ground
and tried to fly in vain
hooks on the legs
cheese on their wings

lipstick stuck to her lips
like taffy on her teeth

don't agree to anything
until the money is not as dirty
as the single broken shoe
on top of the garbage

dimes and nickels
farmer joe was a simpleton
he ate pancakes at dawn
he drank black coffee
he had to move his hat to block the sun
from his face

the tractor is not in use
it hasn't been in two years
the foxes brought their tears of stone
into the fields

realize that the milk is not white
it was orange
just like the twilight
when the cows ate their own brains

Money Rockets

if you deposit a dream
into the bed bank
you will survive the nightmare

if you bought a purse
filled with feathers
sleep will come easily

a rocket flew into the sky
and landed on the moon
she was not pleased about that

a man rushed across the street
and was hit by a bus

the model on the ad bloodied
she never thought she would
have had blood on her forehead

sniff sniff
that pile of dog crap
stepped on once
stepped on twice

revenge of the despondent man
cringing mastiff

God And Migrants

black tea
with sugar and milk

the cat goes hungry
but doesn't everyone?

they pick the lettuce
they pick the strawberries

as the sun goes down
they praise god for another
fruitful endeavor

white stucco houses
with chipped paint on the railing
and a dog or two nipping at the
heels of the naughty children

they open their beers slowly
and say that it was too hot today
but they made money

thank you cesar chavez

the dance lasts all night
and so does the tequila
no work tomorrow
so its ok to have a hangover

she from the garbage cans
he from the weeds growing with
the grass

would they fall in love?
of course they would
and soon
really soon

please forgive god
for giving you a bad experience
as a human
he is mighty but humble
and wishes only the best for you

Color See, Color Do

tongue caught
in a net

the pastel colors
shun the rainbow

five fingers
left hand

four fingers
right hand

a bagel with cream cheese
no onions
no poppy seeds

break the pressure
breathe in the black air

the stars are silent
she exudes a beauty
that was like mona lisa

goats climb the mountainside
rocks clamor

bye bye
to the tomboy
a newspaper article
about abductions

The Mountain

batteries dead
a life lost on the tundra
caribou almost extinct

a tent flaps in the wind
the snow trying to get in
their voices low and slow

a mountain of waste
bottles paper masks

he climbed the highest point
back in the 1950's
with a friend
with a compatriot

now there is only a cave
where one man sits
and waits for death
nobody tries to save him

a fog of the worst kind
collapses around the mind
food doesn't stay down

no sleep
no rest

water is scarce
heat even more scarce
the oxygen is thin

War With Ogres

hot chocolate for breakfast
my springer spaniel
sleeps at my feet

the ogre hasn't called yet
he is the best friend
that i never had

why the green bamboo?
why not the bamboo and teak?

it will always bend
in the washed ocean wind

i am afraid
that my life will be nothing
will i be remembered
for my accomplishments
or will i be a ghost
with no home?

the tank rolls on
the bullets fly
the attack planes roar

i am in a battlefield
of regret
there are no bodies
only dirt and ash

i missed it by
that much
only to see the clouds turn orange
in the night sky

Dirty, Very Dirty

the man was so small
he fell into a covered grate
on the mission street stop
level four

down down he went
so diminished
the rats would eat him
in a second
or maybe two

seaweed
foul smelling water
a floating dog's feces

off to the races
to the end of the line
where the sea met the sewers

he forgot that he was supposed
to turn in his library books
fine- 10 cents a day for each book

the little brain
outsmarted the big brain
because the big brain
didn't use all of its matter

spilled coffee on the lap
the corduroy pants scream
no mercy for white

Deeds Done Silently

fish heads
my brothers
not again not again

the cold soda
poured down
the reluctant throat

they didn't know
it was poisoned
it only took a matter of minutes

the weeds grow higher
and hide the bodies

the sun cooks their
dark skin
flies rejoice in having
more food

a torn collar
on the bloody branch
of a maple tree

he was the only one
who was the coward
he fought the wishes
he fought the caffeine

Mile High Club

he came off the airplane
full of confidence
full of the glow of sex

she waited for him
and waved when she
saw him come into the airport

he weakly smiled
and kissed her on the cheek
what a betrayal
what a betrayal

she knew that he was pure
as pure as the pope in rome

but he still had her stains
on his cheeks
on his pants

thank goodness she couldn't
smell or the perfume
would give him a guilty verdict

thank goodness she was
colorblind or she would see
the rouge in his cheeks

Tough

the boys teased the girls
the same ones who would
be their wives someday

they pulled hair like
pulling a brick of hay from
the tractor

they pulled their panties down
and dropped frogs into them

she was stronger than the rest
she took a stick and pounded them
like a boxer and his punching bag

they ran away
the other girls sighed and
said thank you

but she didn't acknowledge them
because they had been too passive

instead she went into her house
and made some tea
for her mother

mom was a tyrant
she slapped anyone with gum
in their mouths
with the bible

Dizzy Dizzy

wake up
and smell the hanging gardens

bitch about the taste
of bitter coffee

which is it?
the warmth or the cold?

dizzy dizzy
the man is looking
at the wall while the
flies gather around his aura

hello there
welcome to the green zone

saturate the cement
and let it dry in the dangling sun

three times it was not good
four times and it was perfect

looking for susan
she was already down the road
thumbing for rides

the beat of a lion's heart
braver than a soldier
braver than a daredevil

pop pop
the early worms
get the bird

Bock Bock

throbbing pain in my neck
the chicken gets its head cut off

charcoal spider web
flush down the vomit

buzzing enemies
the jungle as thick as
green cotton clouds

pain on
pain off

hemingway was a drunk
but so am i

love is an alien
that takes away the
pain of a thousand pinpricks

scars on the face
scars on the body
a mirror can't discern
the two

skin smells like a
burned out car

beard grows like weeds
with the right amount of light
with the right amount of rain

Full Of Oil And Water

his face cut
his hands ate the weeds

good day to you
you abrasive son of a bitch
you full of oil and water

have some food
i'm not going to eat it
the flies have had their way
with it already

have a drink
i know you want it
sip or gulp
i don't care
poison poison

sit with me under the awning
and yawn songs of sadness
while i kick at the table leg
it needs new bruises

breathe in that smoggy air
it is better than cigarettes
well maybe not
but it will give you what you want

give me the key
to the forbidden triangle
i will keep it safe
until blood drips freely

Kiss The Revolver

the resentment he had for me
was like a tornado ripping
the roofs off houses

she picked me before him
i was the cute one
he was the ground coffee one

he always tore out of the driveway
when i opened the door
and she was there to greet me

he kissed his revolver
waiting for the right day or night
to finally put a bullet into me

the light in the bedroom is off
he takes out the pipe
and stuffs it with the green stuff

smokes a little outside
even the stars weep for him
though he is the most evil of all

he will never forget
the afternoon when she
wanted to go to the circus

you already have a freak with you
he said

she frowned and her hand
was raised to slap him

but she stopped
seeing granite in his eyes

Whistle Sling

game on
the speakers
reiterate the threat
or was it an oath?

cotton candy for hair
two black coals
a red vine smile

pictures in my head
a mirror of her twisted face
sits on my lap

yellow fingernails
dry lips
a pumpkin for a stomach

at least the seats were comfortable
and they brought me food
when i was hungry

but sleep did not come
this evil monday night
he punched his fists into
the thick smoky air

that train ride
with all those negative voices
if god wasn't with me
i would have jumped out the window

assault
physical and emotional
gliding above the talk and insult

Victim Of Vice

such a short time
from fire to water
the sirens screamed like
a wound to the arm

the children laugh
at the wind
because the stench
smells like candy to them

she stared at me
what is it that you want?
a handsome face
or a perfect body?
i have neither

frogs jump from lily to lily
duct tape tongues
as long and elastic as
a bungee cord

they get their fill of flying
insects between twilight
and dusk

uncut fingernails
can't use them with a hammer
only crooked teeth
that are brown to the touch

his mouth liked cigarettes
lips strong as a vice
lungs will fail in 5 years

End Of A Marriage

i don't know if
i should tell her

when i had kidney stones
it felt like she had
kicked me in the back

when i had an aneurysm
it felt like she
poured cold water on my head

when i had gout
she lit fires on my feet

but this
i can't make up my mind

the ring still cold
in my pocket

i wore out my knee
for the right moment

if she turns around
and leaves
i'll probably win over
the bottle of johnny walker

if she stays and kisses me
the gold in her heart
will shine like a lighthouse
in a dense fog

my hands shake
cigarettes will not save me

keep the blue gaze true
let the teeth do the talking
win her
win her

Steve Baba is a poet living in San Francisco. He has taught poetry workshops all over the USA. He calls home NYC, Santa Fe, New Mexico, Honolulu, Hawaii and London, England. Currently working on a memoir based in his time in London, Steve has 10 poetry collections and a collection of short stories published.

www.ingramcontent.com/pod-product-compliance
Lightning Source LLC
Chambersburg PA
CBHW061731020426
42331CB00006B/1190